LEADERSHIP

MATTERS

By

TUNDE JAIYEBO

J-CHARIS MEDIA HOUSE

Published by

J-Charis Media House

Cultural Centre Road, Mokola.

CONTENTS

ABOUT THE AUTHOR

OTHER LEADERSHIP BOOKS BY THE AUTHOR

OTHER BOOKS FROM CHARIS MEDIA HOUSE

CHAPTERONE

LEADERSHIP AND SUCCESS

"Good-tempered leaders invigorate lives; they're like spring rain and sunshine".

Proverbs 16:15. The Message

There is a dire need for men and women, who will take charge, give direction and exert godly influence, thus producing real success in life.

The painful truth however, is that far too many people are so consumed with making a living that the thought of influencing others does not cross their minds. Only a few venture to be leaders. Very few dare to attempt to give direction and exercise godly influence.

For many, the price of leadership is too high hence they are content to be paid rather than pay others; directed rather than give direction; led rather than lead; instructed rather than give instructions. This is why there is a shortage of leaders. But it ought not to be. As a leader, you are therefore, among the top echelon in your chosen field and in life. Leadership makes you a voice. It makes you a reference point. It makes you stand out.

As a leader, God wants you to be duly in charge, faithfully discharging your leadership responsibility and exerting godly influence. Your godly influence is a tool to making those you lead to succeed. God wants you to succeed and make others a success. Success is critical to leadership.

WHAT EXACTLY IS SUCCESS?

God has planted the potential to succeed in every human being. When this potential is not worked out, failure is inevitable. The desire to succeed must be harnessed, developed, worked on and channeled in the right direction and a leader plays a critical role in ensuring that success is achieved.

The big question we need to now answer is "what is success?" If you get the meaning of success wrong, then, you are going to exert your energies, resources and time in the wrong direction and success would remain elusive.

A wrong definition of success will lead to wrong priorities, disappointment, frustration and unhappiness. Living life with a wrong definition of success is like chasing shadows. It is a frustrating experience. It is a life lived under the illusion that one is about to "hit it" but there is nothing to lay hold on.

Many define success as good fortune, prosperity, fame, wealth, status or popularity. This definition is fraught with problems. We have seen so-called successful people who are wealthy but terminally sick. Can this be real success? We have so-called successful people who were famous and influential but committed suicide because they were fed up with life. Can this be the meaning of success? What of the high and mighty, the rich and famous, the respected and the revered, whose homes are in shambles? These definitely cannot be true success.

Success in the before God is all embracing and all encompassing.

Success is accomplishing the totality of God's plan generally as contained in life's manual (the bible) and specifically, by fulfilling God's individual plan for your life. Success, if not well understood by a leader, will lead to lopsided effectiveness. A leader who does not understand the true meaning of success cannot lead others to achieve it.

A leader must have a proper comprehensive understanding of success. Success must be an all-round affair. As a leader, you must not only make an impact with your leadership skills but you must also "do well" in your health, finances, relationships and family life. You must strive to be a true leader indeed.

At no other time in the history of the world has there been so much talk about success, leadership and attainment. People thirst and want to be led in to attain true and lasting success and as a leader, you stand out to meet this need. Many who have "found" themselves in leadership positions have not lived up to expectations, thus dashing the hopes and aspirations of many. A major reason for this is because most of them have a wrong definition and concept of leadership is basically influence. Influence is affecting people's beliefs and actions. Leadership is influencing, affecting people's beliefs and actions to empower them to accomplish divine plans and purposes. Leadership is a divine trust. "Good leadership is a channel of water controlled by God; he directs it to whatever ends he chooses." Proverbs 21:1 The Message.

A DIVINE RESPONSIBILITY

Any leadership journey starts with having a right perspective and an effective utilization of God's endowments.

No man is created empty. Every man is a carrier and custodian of God's investment. To be an effective leader, you have a duty to faithfully utilize the investment of God in your life (gifts, talents, skills, experience, special abilities, potentials etc). You have been endowed by God with various investments and this automatically places on you the responsibility to be a person of influence through the use of these investments. The nature of the believer is to be a source of influence.

"Ye are the salt of the earth: but if the salt have lost his savour, wherewith shall it be salted? It is thenceforth good for nothing, but to be cast out, and to be trodden under foot of men. Ye are the light of the world. A city that is set on a hill cannot be hid. Neither do men light a candle, and put it under a bushel, but on a candlestick; and it giveth light unto all that are in the house. Let your light so shine before men, that they may see your good works, and glorify your Father which is in heaven." **Mathew 5:13-16.**

The Lord Jesus Christ used two metaphors to describe the believer – salt and light.

"Ye are the light of the world" – if we are so described, we need to understand exactly what light is and what it does.

Light is a tool of influence. Light always illuminates - it makes things visible. Light produces direction as it displaces darkness and makes the way obvious. Light is always at its best when it is prominent.

"Ye are the light of the world. A city that is set on a hill cannot be hid. Neither do men light a candle, and put it under a bushel, but on a candlestick; and it giveth light unto all that are in the house." **Mathew. 5:14-15.**

The Lord Jesus ends the illustration of light by giving a command:

"Let your light so shine before men, that they may see your good works, and glorify your Father which is in heaven" **Mathew 5:16.**

Beloved, wherever you find yourself is an opportunity for you to stand out and shine. You have been mandated to have the influence light has. You are the light of the world, so it is your responsibility to shine wherever you are.

"Arise, shine; for thy light is come, and the glory of the LORD is risen upon thee. For, behold, the darkness shall cover the earth, and gross darkness the people: but the LORD shall arise upon thee, and his glory shall be seen upon thee. And the Gentiles shall come to thy light, and kings to the brightness of thy rising." **Isaiah 60:1-3.**

The Lord expects and demands every Christian to "arise and shine". You must understand that your mandate to shine is not for fun. You are to shine so the world – your scope of influence – can experience certain things because of you. *"Let your light so shine before men, that they may see your good works, and glorify your Father which is in heaven".* **Mathew 5:16.** As a child of God, you are to bring glory to God by exhibiting the good works God has ordained you to showcase.

"For we are his workmanship, created in Christ Jesus unto good works, which God hath before ordained that we should walk in them." **Ephesians 2:10.** As a leader, the investment and endowment of God in your life become strategic tools to be used to influence lives and bring glory to God. You are to show the way by your light and give

direction and leadership to others.

The Lord Jesus Christ also describe the believer as salt. Unlike light, which is a visible source of influence, salt is a subtle and invisible source of influence. Salt is a preservative. It prevents the decay and corruption of food. This means wherever you find yourself you must be a preservative agent; your presence must reduce decay and corruption. Your involvement in anything influences it to be preserved.

Salt also is a spice – it brings out the unique flavor in food. You are designed to influence people and organizations to bring out their uniqueness. You bring out the best in people.

Salt sweetens food, so as a believer, your life and work should be a "sweetener".

One does not require a large quantity of salt in order to make the difference in a meal. The implication of this is, that the believer need not be of any particular status or great position to exert influence. Every believer is by nature, a source of influence.

As salt and light, you have the responsibility of being both a visible and an invisible influence. As a leader, you must understand who God has made you to be.

"And the LORD shall make thee the head, and not the tail; and thou shalt be above only, and thou shalt not be beneath; if that thou hearken unto the commandments of the LORD thy God, which I command thee this day, to observe and to do them." **Deuteronomy 28:13.**

You are head and not tail - God expects you to discharge the responsibility of doing everything the head does -

Brain - Thinking (strategizing);

Eyes - Seeing (vision);

Ears - Hearing (perception);

Mouth - Talking (being a voice);

Understanding this responsibility will make you realize that you are a critical factor in influencing people to make a success out of their lives. Leadership is a very powerful tool of influence that must be taken with a great sense of responsibility.

TARGETED LEADERSHIP

Leadership is a serious issue as it relates to and affects lives. Leadership responsibility is not to be exercised in a vacuum. "The mark of a good leader is loyal followers; leadership is nothing without a following." **Proverbs 14:28 The Message.**

Your scope of influence is not for an "all – comers – clubs." You must identify the scope and group of people you are called to influence. Not everybody will appreciate and accept your influence.

If you try to influence (exercise leadership) over people who are not designed to be under the scope of your influence, you are courting trouble. They will stress you. They will not respect you. They will not value you or your time. They will waste your time, energy and resources.

Your leadership influence therefore, must be carefully exercised and not wasted.

"Don't cast your pearls before swine." **Matthew 7:6**

Even the Lord Jesus Christ in His earthly ministry was not sent to everyone.

"But he answered and said, I am not sent but unto the lost sheep of the house of Israel." **Mathew 15:24.**

It is no hidden truth that the Pharisees and top echelon of authority, did not accept the leadership influence of Jesus.

God wants you to discover the people He has sent you to influence. Paul was primarily sent to influence the gentiles and Peter, the Jews.

"Instead, they saw that God had given me the responsibility of preaching the gospel to the Gentiles, just as he had given Peter the responsibility of preaching to the Jews. For the same God who worked through Peter as the apostle to the Jews also worked through me as the apostle to the Gentiles." **Galatians 2:7-8 New Living Translation.**

Success in leadership comes by exercising influence over the right group of people.

LEADERSHIP ON PURPOSE

Leadership cannot be exercised blindly. It must be for specific purposes, goals and aims.

"For Christ didn't send me to baptize, but to preach the Good News--and not with clever speech, for fear that the cross of Christ would lose its power." **1 Corinthians 1:17 New Living Translation.**

A leader must know what his leadership is out to accomplish.

"And he came to Nazareth, where he had been brought up: and, as his custom was, he went into the synagogue on the sabbath day, and stood up for to read, And there was delivered unto him the book of the prophet Esaias. And when he had opened the book, he found the place where it was written, The Spirit of the Lord is upon me, because he hath anointed me to preach the gospel to the poor; he hath sent me to heal the brokenhearted, to preach deliverance to the captives, and re-covering of sight to the blind, to set at liberty them that are bruised, To preach the acceptable year of the Lord, And he closed the book, and he gave it again to the minister, and sat down. And the eyes of all them that were in the synagogue were fastened on him and he began to say unto them, this day is this scripture fulfilled in your ears." **Luke 4:16-21.**

The ultimate purpose of leadership is to help people enter into the fullness of God's plan for their lives, to assist them to be all God wants them to be and to enable them go wherever He wants them to go. In essence, leadership is to make a success of people, bearing in mind that success is accomplishing the totality of

God's plans and purpose. As a leader, you need to step out and take the challenge ahead of you.

Multitudes are waiting for people who will step into leadership positions so they can be given direction. Millions of people are eagerly waiting to come under the umbrella of good leadership and make a success of their lives. The waiting list is endless and it includes individuals, groups, nations, companies etc.

Leadership is a serious issue which must be handled with every sense of seriousness and responsibility. It must be exercised with knowledge.

CHAPTER TWO

INQUISITIVE MIND

"Wise men and women are always learning, always listening for fresh insights."

Proverbs 18:15 The Message.

Information is the currency of the world we live now and if you are to be relevant and useful, you need to acquire information. A leader who is not a perpetual student will soon lose his leadership position. Only the leaders, who are readers, will have an enduring leadership. Leadership demands having a desire to know and make enquiries.

One of the instincts of man is the desire to know. This desire manifests in the form of making enquiries. You will observe that every child loves and easily pops the question "why?" Nobody ever teaches them to ask why; they just manifest this God-given ability to make enquiries. The irony of life is that many parents kill this ability because of ignorance. Many parents berate their children for poking into their business; they shut them up for talking too much, and they shout them down for asking too many questions. Therefore, many children are brought up with their "enquiry mind" suppressed or even killed. The desire to know why is crushed. The eagerness to discover "how- come" is strangled. The desire to want to know more than meets the eye is aborted. The quest for adventure is starved to death. We now have a generation that just accepts whatever they see without complaint.

They have lost the ability to ask why and they cannot be bothered to ask why not either.

Making enquiries makes you look like a fool but after sensibly applying the results of your enquiry, you will become wise in a short time. It is better to look like a fool for five minutes than to become a fool forever! Nothing should stop you from making enquiries. When you become too old or you think you are too young to ask questions, you are on the slippery road to mediocrity. When you think you know too much or you are above making enquiries, then, you are limiting your progress. Nobody has a monopoly of knowledge. As long as you are on this side of eternity, you are always in school asking and receiving answers.

"Anyone who claims to know all the answers doesn't really know much." **1 Corinthians 8:2 New Living Translation.**

A man who is not learning is as good as dead. A leader who is not learning is not fit for the office he holds. It is sad and it is a disaster to have a leader who has no desire and time to learn. A leader who will not be open to new ideas is a misfit in that office.

"The intelligent man is open to new ideas, in fact he looks for them." **Proverbs 18:15 New Living Translation**

People who have made enduring impact in life have been men and women who were avid readers and learners.

Our society has turned things upside down. We have put the cart before the horse. We have been brought up to think that we go to school to learn and get a qualification; after which we are delivered from the rigors of learning. No wonder we have graduates today who pride themselves in their paper qualification(s) but are total illiterates.

May I ask you some questions – how many books have you read this year? Do you have a desire to make enquiries in what you do? Do you make effort to go the extra mile to acquire knowledge? What new method have you learnt in the last six months to make your job done better? Can you describe yourself as a learner? How do you respond to new ideas?

We are encouraged to study as an antidote for shame:

"Study to shew thyself approved unto God, a workman that needeth not to be ashamed, rightly dividing the word of truth." **2 Timothy 2:15**

Life is a school you do not graduate from. A fool is someone who has no desire for knowledge.

"It is senseless to pay tuition for a fool who has no heart for wisdom." **Proverbs 17:16 New Living Translation.**

We live in what is now referred to as the information age. The world is ruled and governed by information. A leader who has no access to information is completely cut off. A leader who does not update himself will soon find out that he will be out of date. A leader who does not know the value, use and relationship between the computer and his work would be out of the market place in the next few years.

Your desire must always be to make enquiries from books, lectures, seminars, people, the internet etc.

Leadership is more than occupying an office, having a status or having an exalted position. Leadership is work. Leadership is providing direction. Leadership is giving insight and helping the people move from their present to their future.

For any leader to succeed, he must be able to provide answers to some specific questions. There will be certain pertinent questions that will arise in the course of the leadership journey. These questions will relate to his person and personality and will also relate to the organization he is a leader over. The accurate answer to these questions will determine how far a leader will succeed and take the organization he leads to. These questions are basic, simple and common but the answers have far reaching effects.

The answer to these questions can be the difference between success and failure, survival or going under, profit or loss, strangulation or expansion. The answer to these questions are fundamental for survival in this very competitive world, where people have multiple choices.

CHAPTERTHREE

CRITICAL QUESTION; "WHY?"

"The wise are known for their understanding, and pleasant words are persuasive."

Proverbs 16:2 New Living Translation.

The days of "anything goes" are over. Only organizations with clearly defined and identifiable objectives, workable strategies, relevant and useful products/services will find acceptability, patronage and profitability. As a leader you must understand this. You must provide answer to certain critical questions. The first question, and the most crucial, is why. You will need to ask and clearly answer the question why. Why answers the question of purpose, the reason the organization you are leading is in existence. Why is your company in business? Why was your organization formed? Why are you involved in the banking sector of the economy and not the insurance sector? Why has your department in the office been created? Why are you doing what you are doing the way you do it? Why are you located where you are? Why?

A leader that cannot clearly answer the question "why" cannot survive for too long. An organization must be known for something, whether it be a club, church, charitable organization or company. When you find the answer to the question why, then, you can properly articulate your vision and mission statement. Vision is the picture of a preferred future. Vision is the product of divine insight and since only God knows the future, He alone can give us a picture of it. Vision is not and should not be a contraption of your imagination or ambition but the result of a discourse with God.

Let us see some principles of vision from Habakkuk 2:1-4: "I will stand upon my watch, and set me upon the tower, and will watch to see what he will say unto me, and what I shall answer when I am reproved, And the LORD answered me, and said, Write the vision, and make it plain upon tables, that he may run that readeth it, For the vision is yet for an appointed time, but at the end it shall speak, and not lie: though it tarry, wait for it; because it will surely come, it will not tarry, Behold, his soul which is lifted up is not upright in him: but the just shall live by his faith."

A true vision is birthed in the place of prayer and in discussion with God (the one who knows the future). *"I will stand upon my watch, and set me upon the tower, and will watch to see what he will say unto me, and what I shall answer when I am reproved."* **Habakkuk 2:1.**

A true vision must be written plainly for people who read it to understand it. *"And the LORD answered me, and said, Write the vision, and make it plain upon tables, that he may run that readeth it."* **Verse2.**

A true vision should be clearly caught by its target audience. " *... That he may run that reads it".* **Verse 2**

A true vision is time based. "For the vision is yet for an appointed time." Verse3a.

A true vision will eventually be realized in its fullest form over time *"For the vision is yet for an appointed time, but at the end it shall speak, and not lie: though it tarry, wait for it; because it will surely come, it will not tarry."* **Verse 3.**

A true vision will demand faith for it to be executed. *"Behold, his soul which is lifted up is not upright in him: but the just shall live by his faith."* **Verse 4.**

Your vision as a leader tells the whole world, why you are in existence. The answer to the question why should be the parameter to determine the things your group or your organization can do and cannot do. The answer to the question why is what makes you differ from the organization next door. The answer to the question why will eliminate competitive jealousy, pride and duplication of resources. The answer to the question why enables those involved in the organization you lead to have focus and set their attention and resources in the same direction. The answer to the question why will guide in the setting of goals.

A good leader fully understands the why of his organization. He has a clear understanding of the why, so he can map out the necessary strategies to get the job done.

When you understand the way of the group which you lea, you become better positioned to influence your members to achieve the purpose of the group.

In actual fact, the job of the leader is simply to influence his team to fulfil the why of the existence of the organization. Answering the question why will help the leader spell out the necessary steps and strategy needed to implement and execute her purpose. Since the answer to the question why is the reason for the existence of the organization, and since the leader is the person to ensure this purpose is accomplished, you as a leader, hold a very strategic position.

To be an effective and successful leader, you need to do a self-appraisal regularly by asking and answering the following questions – What qualifies me to get the purpose of this organization fulfilled? Qualification to get the job done is not limited to "paper" qualifications, it also includes your gifting, your grace, your anointing, your psychological and emotional make-up, interpersonal and organizational skills etc. These "non–paper" qualifications are particularly important when you want to answer the question "who" and "who with", which is the next question to ask after sorting out why. The answer to the question why will determine the kind and calibre of staff you will need to recruit.

CHAPTER FOUR

CRITICAL QUESTION; "WHO?"

"The mark of a good leader is loyal followers; leadership is nothing without a following."

Proverbs 14:28 The Message.

Nothing big or significant can be accomplished single-handedly; people have to be involved one way or the other. People have to be involved either as partners, buyers, distributors, staff, church members, employers, financiers, end-users or recipients of a service or product etc. That is why you must ask and answer the pertinent question: who?

The question of who deals with personnel; it deals with people. It involves you asking: who will get the job done? Who will facilitate the execution of your dream? Who do you need to help you with the job? What aspects of the job do you need people to be involved? What kind of people do you need to assist you? Whom will the job have an effect on?

In essence, the question who provokes an enquiry as to the people whom you, as a matter of necessity, have to be involved with directly or indirectly in the execution of your responsibility as a leader or in the realization of your dream (whether it be a ministry, business, career, special project, academics, marriage etc).

When you have a dream, you cannot execute it alone, whether the dream is to build a great business or to take your organization to the next level or for your organization to become the pacesetter or the market leader or to build a great family or to pastor a great church, you need people. You need a team and network of people.

A good team allows for specialization and greater efficiency. It enables and frees the members to focus on, develop and contribute to the advancement of the overall team in their area of strength and specialization. A good team is known by its diversity - the members are not the same kind of people. They are people with different areas of specialization. The vision and purpose of their coming together is the same, but their inputs are not the same. Each is bringing in his own individual and specialized contribution. No member of the team is a duplication of the other:

"For the body is not one member, but many. If the foot shall say, be-

cause I am not the hand, I am not of the body; is it therefore not of the body? And if the ear shall say, because I am not the eye, I am not of the body; is it therefore not of the body? If the whole body were an eye, where were the hearing? If the whole were hearing, where were the smelling? But now hath God set the members every one of them in the body, as it hath pleased him. And if they were all one member, where were the body? But now are they many members, yet but one body. And the eye cannot say unto the hand, I have no need of thee: nor again the head to the feet, I have no need of you." **1Corinthians 12:14-21.**

A team that has every member having the same skills, same qualifications and specializations is not a team but a club! A good team is one that consists of different people with different traits, talents, viewpoints, backgrounds, exposures and experiences. The team members complement each other - where one is weak, another is strong, where one does not have the expertise, another has. Their coming together therefore means that the collective body has no weaknesses.

Understanding the question who will greatly assist a leader in assigning duties (delegation). It will also help in how he will relate to his colleagues and subordinates (relationships). In addition, it will equip the leader to know where to direct resources and opportunities for developing the unique gifts of his team (leadership and skill development and deployment).

The second benefit of a good team is, as the saying goes, "two heads are better than one":

"It is better to have a partner than to go it alone. Share the work, share the wealth. And if one falls down, the other helps. But if there's no one to help, tough!" **Ecclesiastes 4:9-10 The Message.**

"Two people are better off than one, for they can help each other succeed. If one person falls, the other can reach out and help. But someone who falls alone is in real trouble." **Ecclesiastes 4:9-10 New Living Translation.**

A good team reduces overwork and burnout. When a leader or an organization does not have a good team, there is always the problem of people getting overworked. When a leader cannot take a break from his work for some time, it shows clearly that he does not have a good team or he has been failing/neglecting to delegate.

When a leader or a key figure in the organization seems indispensable and cannot go on vacation, it is a clear sign that a good and effective team is lacking. It also shows that there is an inadequate leadership development programme. A leader cannot be at more than one place at once. However, if he has a good team, he can "multiply" himself through his team to be at many places at the same time.

CHAPTERFIVE

CRITICAL QUESTION; "WHO WITH?"

*"It's better to have a partner than go it
alone. Share the work, share the wealth.
And if one falls down, the other helps, But
if there's no one to help, tough!"*

Ecclesiastes 4:9-10 The Message.

nother pertinent questions that must be dealt with in the journey of success for a leader is the question who with?

Who with is a step deeper than the question who. While the question who, deals with the general dimension of people who have an impact /contribution to the execution of your dream, the who with question goes deeper. Who with deals with the people who are directly involved in the execution of your dream.

There are many angles to this question; but we will look at it from that of the people who have to work directly with the leader. We will look at the delegation of your work to these sets of people. Someone said, if you want a job to be done well, do it yourself but if you want a job to last, then delegate it.

Delegation is the act and the art of entrusting and conferring authority to a subordinate to act on your behalf. The mere giving, issuing or barking out instructions to get something done is not delegation!

A crucial and indispensable ingredient of delegation is the granting of authority. Authority must be granted to the "delegate" (the person you are delegating to) to enforce decisions and to use his/her discretion as to how to get the job done within specified guidelines.

Authority must be delegated but accountability cannot be delegated. Accountability always rests with the leader or the person delegating. The buck always ends at your table as the leader. The leader takes responsibility for the actions/inactions of his team. A good leader takes responsibility for the action and inactions of his who with. This is why answering the question who with is very fundamental. When you effectively answer the question who with, you would find out that delegating work/responsibility to them will yield exceptional results.

"And in those days, when the number of the disciples was multiplied,

there arose a murmuring of the Grecians against the Hebrews, because their widows were neglected in the daily ministration. Then the twelve called the multitude of the disciples unto them, and said, It is not reason that we should leave the word of God, and serve tables. Wherefore, brethren, look ye out among you seven men of honest report, full of the Holy Ghost and wisdom, whom we may appoint over this business. But we will give ourselves continually to prayer, and to the ministry of the word. And the saying pleased the whole multitude: and they chose Stephen, a man full of faith and of the Holy Ghost, and Philip, and Prochorus, and Nicanor, and Timon, and Parmenas, and Nicolas a proselyte of Antioch: Whom they set before the apostles: and when they had prayed, they laid their hands on them. And the word of God increased; and the number of the disciples multiplied in Jerusalem greatly; and a great company of the priests were obedient to the faith." **Acts 6:1-7.**

We can see some crucial points from the above scripture reference.

1. The greater the number of people being led, the more complicated things will be if care is not taken. **(Verse 1).**

2. Crises must not take the leader from his primary assignment or purpose. **(Verse 2).**

3. Set standards and qualification must be in place before appointing people into offices. **(Verse 3).**

4. Leaders must give themselves continually to their primary purpose and not lose focus. (Verse 4).

5. Good leadership will motivate and move the followers into positive actions. **(Verse 5).**

6. Appointment to offices should be made public and the people divinely empowered to carry out their set assignments. **(Verse 6).**

7. Effective leadership through discovering, empowering and re-

leasing the who and the who with will always produce results and move the organization forward. **(Verse 7).**

CUT DOWN
YOUR COST

The fact that you can delegate routine tasks which seem challenging to your who with, frees you to face other critical and major assignments.

Delegating work to your who with also reduces costs because the lower the level at which a job is done, the cheaper it costs. Let me give an example: when a manager who earns two hundred thousand naira a month employs and delegates the time-consuming aspect of his work that deals with collecting, collating and typing of data to a qualified fresh computer graduate, who is paid fifty thousand naira a month, that job is definitely done cheaper. The manager can then devote his time to other important aspects of his job and give just a fraction of his time to supervise the fresh graduate's work.

When you discover and delegate work to your who with in your establishment, you are contributing to his leadership development and increasing his value, consequently making him more useful to your organization and society.

When you don't answer the question who with, there are tell-tale signs that will be visible. When you find it difficult to meet deadlines and you have a pile of unfinished work, it is very probable that you are biting more than you can chew and you are not delegating. When you spend too much time looking over the shoulders of your workers, it is most probable that you are either working with the wrong set people or you have not trained them well.

When you effectively answer the question who with, you will need not spend too much time wondering, sneaking and watching over your shoulders. They will be the right people for you to work with in the execution of your dream, project, assignment or task.

When you spend time doing for others what they can do for themselves, you have not discovered or you are not utilizing the answer to your who with question.

People who look invincible and seemingly indispensable due to keeping close to their chest things which need not be secret find it difficult to delegate.

Your answering the question who with is indispensable to your success. Many have their dreams truncated because they were not able to locate their - who with. Others, who discovered their who with and did not relate to them well are today telling tales of woe and regret. You need to sit down and do a thorough analysis of your job/assignment and find out what you have to do yourself and what you have to delegate. Bad leadership is when one man is doing everybody's job.

Prayerfully look for the answer to the who with to effectively get the job done with you and for you.

To facilitate your getting the right people to work with you as a leader, you must clearly understand the qualifications of the people you need. *"Wherefore, brethren, look ye out among you seven men of honest report, full of the Holy Ghost and wisdom, whom we may appoint over this business"* **Act6:3.**

When there is ambiguity on the calibre and qualifications of people you want to work with, you will end up working with the wrong people who will hinder your effectiveness. In dealing with the answer to your who with, you must know and operate on the biblical standard relating to employee-employer/employer-employee relationship.

"Servants, be obedient to them that are your masters according to the flesh, with fear and trembling, in singleness of your heart, as unto Christ; Not with eye service, as menpleasers; but as the servants of Christ, doing the will of God from the heart; With good will doing service, as to the Lord, and not to men:

Knowing that whatsoever good thing any man doeth, the same shall he receive of the Lord, whether he be bond or free. And, ye masters, do the same things unto them, forbearing threatening: knowing that your Master also is in heaven; neither is there respect of persons with him." **Ephesians 6:5-9.**

"Servants, obey in all things your masters according to the flesh; not with eyeservice, as menpleasers; but in singleness of heart, fearing God: And whatsoever ye do, do it heartily, as to the Lord, and not unto men; Knowing that of the Lord ye shall receive the reward of the inheritance: for ye serve the Lord Christ." Colossians 3:22-24.

God expects justice, fairness and equity in the employer- employee relationship.

"Masters give unto your servants that which is just and equal; knowing that ye also have a Master in heaven." **Colossians 4:1.**

In addition, the bible clearly outlines qualifications of leaders.

"This is a true saying, if a man desires the office of a bishop, he desireth a good work. A bishop then must be blameless, the husband of one wife, vigilant, sober, of good behaviour, given to hospitality, apt to teach; Not given to wine, no striker, not greedy of filthy lucre; but patient, not a brawler, not covetous;

One that ruleth well his own house, having his children in subjection with all gravity; (For if a man know not how to rule his own house, how shall he take care of the church of God?) Not a novice, lest being lifted up with pride he fall into the condemnation of the devil. Moreover he must have a good report of them which are without; lest he fall into reproach and the snare of the devil." **1 Timothy 3:1-7.**

Paul re-echoes these qualifications to Titus.

"But a lover of hospitality, a lover of good men, sober, just, holy, temperate; If any be blameless, the husband of one wife, having faithful children not accused of riot or unruly. For a bishop must be blameless, as the steward of God; not self-willed, not soon angry, not given to wine, no striker, not given to filthy lucre; But a lover of hospitality, a lover of good men, sober, just, holy, temperate; Holding fast the faithful word as he hath been taught, that he may be able by sound doctrine both to exhort and to convince the gainsayers." **Titus 1:5-9.**

You will notice these qualifications can be divided into three major categories: competence, character and family.

One would have thought that competence should be the major qualification which should be emphasized but it is not so.

Under competence, there are four basic qualifications – (1) apt to teach (2) one that ruleth well his own house (3) not a novice (4) steadfast in the faith. *"A man who takes his stand on orthodox faith, so that he can by sound teaching both stimulate faith and confute opposition"* **Titus 1:8 Phillips.**

Concerning family we have: (1) Husband of one wife (2) having his children in subjection and all gravity (well trained and behaved children).

For character, we have: (1) blameless (without reproach, a life that cannot be spoken against) (2) vigilant (3) sober (cool, calm and calculated; exhibiting self-control) (4) good behavior (dignified, respectable, composed, serious) (5) good report of them that are without (reputation) (6) not a stricker/brawler (averse to strife, not quarrelsome, not violent, combative to given to blows) (7) not greedy of filthy lucre and not coveteous (not making money through dishonest or dishonourable means) (8) not self-willed (not stubborn) (9) patient (10) not given to wine (11) not soon angry (12) just (morally right and fair, ethical, honest and principled) (13) Devout (earnestly sincere, God-fearing) (14) temperate (self-controlled and disciplined) (15) given to hospitality (16) holy (17) lover of goodmen (right and holy living).

I believe the reason we have more character requirements than competence and family is because character is the foundation upon which competence and the family stand. Once the foundation of character cracks, competence and family will eventually crumble.

"Moral character makes for smooth traveling; an evil life is a hard life. Good character is the best insurance; crooks get trapped in their sinful lust." Proverbs **11:5-6 The Message.** *"Good leaders abhor wrongdoing of all kinds; sound leadership has a moral foundation."* **Proverbs 16:12 The Message.**

Great care must be taken not to give undue precedence and prominence to competence and charismas at the expense of character.

"Be wary of false preachers who smile a lot, dripping with practiced sincerity. Chances are they are out to rip you off some way or other. Don't be impressed with charisma; look for character." **Matthew 7:15 The Message**.

If you want your leadership to be an enduring one with maximum impact, you must develop your character. Competence will make you climb to the zenith of whatever you do, but it is character that will keep you there. A competent leader without good character is a disaster waiting to happen.

Character is the distinctive nature of a Christian. It is the manifestation of the fruit of the Spirit:

"But the fruit of the [Holy] Spirit [the work which His presence within accomplishes] is love, joy (gladness), peace, patience (an even temper, forbearance), kindness, goodness (benevolence), faithfulness, Gentleness (meekness, humility), self-control (self- restraint, continence). Against such things there is no law [that can bring a charge]." **Galatians 5:22-23 Amplified.**

CHAPTER SIX

CRITICAL QUESTION; "HOW?"

"The LORD says, "I will guide you along the best pathway for your life. I will advise you and watch over you. Do not be like a senseless horse or mule that needs a bit and bridle to keep it under control."

Psalm 32:8-9 New Living Translation.

We have seen that success in life and in leadership is hinged heavily on asking and answering the right questions. A man who fails to ask questions will languish in the wilderness of ignorance and be banished to the land of non- achievers. We have already looked at three of the questions that must be answered accurately.

One other pertinent question you must strive to ask whenever you have an idea, dream or project is "how?" The answers to the question how is relevant, useful and indispensable to the successful execution of any project. Without asking and answering the question how, it will be practically impossible to map out the necessary strategies for the implementation and execution of any project.

To successfully answer the question how, you will need to have answered the question what; you should have known exactly what you want to do.

Your intended purpose must be clearly spelt out. Once you decide what you want accomplished, then, you need to assess your present position vis-à-vis where you are going.

You will need to do a self-analysis by answering the following questions: What are my qualifications? Am I qualified to execute the purpose, plans and objectives of the organization? Am I competent to get the job done? If I am not, what do I need to do?

Answering the question how simply involves formulating strategy. Most organizations fail because of inadequate or outdated strategy.

The first thing to do when you have a project or an idea is not to start off but to sit down and formulate a strategy.

"Is there anyone here who, planning to build a new house, doesn't first sit down and figure the cost so you'll know if you can complete it? If you only get the foundation laid and then run out of money, you're going to look pretty foolish. Everyone passing by will poke fun at you: 'He

started something he could not finish'." **Luke 14:28-30 The Message.**

The first step in the execution of a project is to "sit down first". Never jump into executing your idea, dream and plans without first taking time out to sit down, settle down and pray. Pray and think, think and plan, think and strategize. A successful project is not the product of good intentions only, it is the product of a well thought out, well articulated and a well executed strategy. The road to hell, they say, is paved with good intentions. Answering the question how involves spending quality time thinking, praying as well as consulting books and people. Consulting God is critical here. God is willingly, able and ready to guide you and this is a very valuable assistance when formulating strategy. You will save yourself a lot of headache if you seek God's guidance and help.

"I will instruct thee and teach thee in the way which thou shalt go: I will guide thee with mine eye. Be ye not as the horse, or as the mule, which have no understanding: whose mouth must be held in with bit and bridle, lest they come near unto thee." Psalm 32: 8-9.

The Holy Spirit is always ready to help.

"Howbeit when he, the Spirit of truth, is come, he will guide you into all truth: for he shall not speak of himself; but whatsoever he shall hear, that shall he speak: and he will shew you things to come." **John 16:13.**

Answering the question how involves counting the cost. Counting the cost is not only a monetary issue but it includes mapping out strategies that will take care of other elements/factors like time, personnel, premises, resources, skill etc. In essence, you are asking what exactly is needed to get the job done? Who and what do I have now? Will what I have be enough to get the job done? How can I equip myself to get the job done? This is what we call planning.

"My child, don't lose sight of good planning and insight. Hang on to them, for they will fill you with life and bring you to honor and respect. They keep you safe on your way and keep your feet from stumbling. You can lie down without fear and enjoy pleasant dreams." **Proverbs 3:21-24 New Living Translation.**

A very important thing to put in mind is this: strategy has to be changed over time and with time.

The answer to the question what, which deals with your vision/mission/assignment, is always constant but the answer to the question how, which deals with strategy is never constant.

Your strategy must be adjusted to suit the environment you find yourself and the environment keeps changing. The economic climate three years ago is not the same today. When people stick to old strategies, they run their business down and they transfer it to the museum. For example, you cannot stick to the strategy of using a typewriter to get your typing jobs done when we now have computers.

"Change is the law of life and those who look only to the past or present are certain to miss the future." - John F. Kennedy.

"He that will not apply new remedies must expect new evils; for time is the greatest innovator." - Francis Bacon.

CHAPTER SEVEN

THE CHALLENGE OF CHANGE

"Intelligent people are always ready to learn. Their ears are open for knowledge."

Proverbs 18:15 New Living Translation.

Change is an integral and indispensable part of life. A good leader, therefore, must know what, where, when and how change is relevant and effected. A leader should be a good arbiter knowing what can be changed and what should not be changed. He also must have the boldness to act on his convictions when the need for change arises. He must not be resistant to change. He must be a good change manager.

"If in the last few years, you haven't discarded a major opinion or acquired a new one, check your pulse, you may be dead." - Gilette Burgess.

A good leader must have the "people skills" to get the people to go along with him in the journey of change.

The fact that change is an inevitable fact of life does not give the leader the liberty to introduce change for the sake of change or just that he might appear "innovative".

A good leader is consistent. Even when a leader makes changes, there is an element of consistency that will be seen by the people (the change should not paint him as a man that has lost direction).

If a leader makes changes that do not achieve the desired results, he stands the risk of his followers losing confidence in him and making them extremely wary next time he wants to introduce another change.

The human nature resists change. People detest and fight change. The average person fears change because it compels him to leave his comfort zone into a new territory. The uncertainty of the new territory, moving from the familiar to the unfamiliar, moving from the usual to the unusual, moving from the known to the unknown is a journey many are not willing to take.

This makes change a big challenge to a leader and for him to successfully navigate the group through change, he must be trusted (as a person, leader and as someone who knows what he is doing). He must develop and use tact when dealing with change. He must be a good manager of change.

"Change has a bad reputation in our society. But it isn't all bad — not by any means. In fact, change is necessary in life — to keep us moving to keep us growing to keep us interested. Imagine life without change. It would be static...boring...and dull." - Dr. Dennis O'Grady.

Change, however, is a proof of growth.

"One key to successful leadership is continuous personal change. Personal change is a reflection of our inner growth and empowerment." - Robert E. Quinn.

We will look at some areas where change is an unlikely event and areas where change should be a common occurrence and a regular feature.

UNLIKELY CHANGE AREAS

A God-given vision is constant. God does not change and He doesn't change his mind about the assignments He gives us.

"For the gifts and calling of God are without repentance." **Romans 11:29.**

A vision can be streamlined and further evolve, but the essence and core of it never changes. Your vision is God's painting of your future: It defines, declares and delineates your assignment. It tells the people why you are their leader. It tells them what their future will look like.

Your vision is your God-given blueprint and roadmap for your leadership journey.

To change the vision is to change direction completely. However, if you know your vision was not from God, then be bold enough to admit your error and change so you can accomplish His will for your life. As Christians, we are bound and guided by God's Word, the Bible.

THE DO-OR-DIE CONVICTION

The Bible is the eternal and immutable word of God. If the word of God cannot change and if the content of our message is the word of God, then, our message too should not change. As a leader, you must be committed to God's word.

A leader should always be committed to the execution of his God-given vision and this commitment should be constant and unchangeable. Commitment is a do- or-die conviction to get the job done. It is a for-better- for-worse attitude to getting the job done. Without commitment, purposes and plans will be frustrated. Commitment is what will keep one going on to the very end.

"And it came to pass, that, as they went in the way, a certain man said unto him, Lord, I will follow thee whithersoever thou goest, And Jesus said unto him, Foxes have holes, and birds of the air have nests; but the Son of man hath not where to lay his head. And he said unto another, Follow me. But he said, Lord, suffer me first to go and bury my father. Jesus said unto him, Let the dead bury their dead: but go thou and preach the kingdom of God. And another also said, Lord, I will follow thee; but let me first go bid them farewell, which are at home at my house. And Jesus said unto him, No man, having put his hand to the plough, and looking back, is fit for the kingdom of God." **Luke 9:57-62.**

Integrity and character are big issues in leadership. As Christians and as leaders who are Christians, we must be known for our unchanging character of integrity, honesty, hard work and exemplary lifestyle – this should be the hallmark and it should never

TUNDE JAIYEBO

change.

INTELLIGENT PEOPLE ARE OPEN TO NEW IDEAS

Times are changing, so must your strategy. Vision and commitment to execute the vision are constant but the strategy to get the job done has to be changed regularly. We preach the same old gospel message but the strategy we use has to be changed regularly.

We cannot use the same old style, channels and methods that were used five years ago to do the same thing in the 21st century.

Strategy is the plan by which the vision is carried out or by which the message is passed across. Strategy deals with the "how to". The "how to" of yesteryears will definitely be obsolete and ineffective today, therefore, we need change.

If you refuse to change your strategy, you will soon be out of date, irrelevant and rendered ineffective.

"Change in the local church is no longer an option, it is a necessity. Modern man feels a gap between the world of the church and the outside world. The world is changing rapidly and the present day church with its rigidity in form cannot cope with that changing world. We must be ready to face a changing world with a changing church." - Lloyd Perry.

Implementing a strategy requires change and change demands asking the following questions, among other questions:

What needs to be done?

What is working now?

What is not working?

What can be done to make what is not working to work?

What actions can be taken to get the job done the way it ought to be done?

In essence, an effective leader constantly courts change by re-assessing, re-evaluating and adapting new strategies to execute the vision. You have to be open to new ideas. What you need to know is determined by those you want to influence. If you want to increase your influence base you will need to, in many cases, overhaul your knowledge base.

"Intelligent people are always open to new ideas. In fact they look for them". **Proverbs 18:15 New Living Translation.**

You must maximize every available source to acquire knowledge:

Invest in books – regularly visit bookshops and buy relevant books and materials.

Attend seminars, conferences, training, and workshops that will sharpen your skills

Have a mentoring/apprenticeship programme. You must be hungry to acquire knowledge. You must learn from every available source. People are books you must read as each life is a message – a lesson on wisdom or foolishness. *"Buy the truth, and sell it not; also wisdom, and instruction, and understanding."* **Proverbs 23:23.**

To maximize your leadership effectiveness, you need to embrace technology which is ever changing. Mike Murdock lists the many benefits of using appropriate technology, among which are:

1. Machines do not require coaxing, just repair;

2. Machines do not get discouraged when their mother-in-law comes to town;

3 Machines are never disloyal, discussing your secrets with every-one else;

4. Your machine will not file grievance report against you when you fail to meet their expectations;

5. Machines do not require medical insurance, sick leave or time off;

6. Machines can be replaced quickly and easily without breaking your heart;

7. Machines never come to work late and want to leave early;

8. Machines will work through lunch, requiring no break time.

A leader must know the appropriate technology needed to execute his leadership.

CHAPTER EIGHT

HOW DO YOU LOOK IN THE MIRROR?

"Don't become so well-adjusted to your culture that you fit into it without even thinking. Instead, fix your attention on God. You'll be changed from the inside out. Readily recognize what he wants from you, and quickly respond to it. Unlike the culture around you, always dragging you down to its level of immaturity, God brings the best out of you, develops well-formed maturity in you."

Romans 12:2 The Message.

Leadership will put you in public glare. You become the cynosure of eyes and target of public opinion. As a leader, if you are to make an impact with your life and exert great influence, then, you must learn to have a healthy self-esteem. Everything is designed to keep you limited but your mind must be made up not to be swallowed up by the spirit of limitation.

Never succumb to the pressure people and society will bring your way. The world wants to squeeze you into a mold and if you refuse, you will be badly labelled.

You must be resolute to be whom God says you are.

"Do not be conformed to this world (this age), [fashioned after and adapted to its external, superficial customs], but be transformed (changed) by the [entire] renewal of your mind [by its new ideals and its new attitude], so that you may prove [for yourselves] what is the good and acceptable and perfect will of God, even the thing which is good and acceptable and perfect [in His sight for you]." **Romans 12:2 Amplified.**

You will come across such statements as "it has never been done", "you are too young", "you are too inexperienced", "The stakes are too high." etc.

History is full of people who went against popular opinion to make indelible marks on the sands of time. Public opinion, criticism, your experiences and exposure to and in life are all tools that can destroy your self-esteem, if care is not taken.

Self-esteem is the basis of your being and your identity. It is the essence and substance of who you are. Self-esteem must be built on the right foundation, else, it collapses when it matters most. A self-esteem founded, premised, based and hinged on material things is risky.

When your self–esteem emanates from material things: money, popularity, possessions or from status, position, association, name or education, you stand the risk of it crashing when these things are adversely affected. Coming against them will be tantamount to coming against you.

It is foolhardy to allow external issues to define, determine or influence your self-esteem and your identity. What you do or don't do should not determine or define who you are. What people say or don't say should not be a determinant of your person and identity. You are who God says you are. You can do what God says you can do. You can be who God says you can be. When you know you are who God says you are, you become delivered from being tossed 'to and fro' by the opinion of people. This is the key to freedom from being ruled by the whims and caprices of people, especially malicious critics.

If what people say is correct (that is valid criticism), you should adjust and make amends but when their criticisms are unfair, malicious and unwarranted, you should ignore it and move on with life. You must see such criticisms as distractions not worthy of your time, energy and attention.

A person whose self–esteem is based on people's opinion will be an emotionally imbalanced person because people's opinion are never constant. Those that cry "Hosanna" today will shout "crucify him" tomorrow.

To have a healthy self-esteem, you must realize that you are significant.

You are here on earth on an assignment and you are the best man for the job - any other person is at best the second best!

You might not measure up now, but God is still working on you. Each one of us is a work in progress under God.

"For God is working in you, giving you the desire and the power to do what pleases him." **Philippians 2:13 New Living Translation.**

When you understand this, you will face life with a positive attitude. How you see yourself (your self-esteem) helps determine how far you will go in life.

Evidence of Low Self-Esteem:

1. Undue attention to people's opinion;

2. Indecision and indecisiveness;

3. Being unduly intimidated and having undue fear of people (their status, opinion etc);

4. Fear of making mistakes;

5. Fear of success;

6. Undue desire to please people;

7. Taking criticisms personal;

8. Making judgments based on comparison;

9. Not wanting to hurt people (usually evidenced by the inability to say 'no' which leads to you making unnecessary sacrifice).

Self-esteem is crucial and you cannot afford to be like everybody else.

"Don't become so well-adjusted to your culture that you fit into it without even thinking. Instead, fix your attention on God. You'll be changed from the inside out. Readily recognize what he wants from you, and quickly respond to it. Unlike the culture around you, always dragging you down to its level of immaturity,

God brings the best out of you, develops well-formed maturity in you." **Romans 12:2 The Message.**

UNIQUE FLAVOUR

A healthy self-esteem will help you to be bold, to stand out and live the unique life God has planned for you. A healthy self-esteem is indispensable for you to be a successful leader. You need it to bless this world with the unique flavor which only you can produce. There is something about you that is unique. There is something about you that nobody else has. There is something about you that cannot be got anywhere else. You are unique, one-of-a-kind; you are special, peculiar and outstanding. There is a unique flavour about you that the world needs. There is a quality peculiar to you and you alone. You must discover, develop and deploy your unique flavour.

If you do what everybody does, you will get the result everybody gets. If you do ordinary things, you will get ordinary results and live an ordinary life. However, if you do things in the area of your uniqueness, you will get unique results and live a unique life. To get unusual results, you must do unusual things. There is something unusual about you that nobody has, which the world needs.

There is something peculiar about you. You have been designed to be different.

"Thank you for making me so wonderfully complex! Your workmanship is marvelous--how well I know it. You watched me as I was being formed in utter seclusion, as I was woven together in the dark of the womb. You saw me before I was born. Every day of my life was recorded in your book. Every moment was laid out before a single day had passed." **Psalm 139:14-16 New Living Translation.**

You are not an accident; neither are you a product of mass production. God uniquely created you with individual attention and specification.

"You know me inside and out, you know every bone in my body; you know exactly how I was made, bit by bit, how I was sculpted from nothing into something. Like an open book, you watched me grow from conception to birth; all the stages of my life were spread out before you, the days of my life all prepared before I'd even lived one day." **Psalm 139:15-16 The Message.**

Scientifically it has been proven that each person is unique. Your fingerprint is unique to you. Your tongue print is like nobody else's. No two human outer ears (even your own right or left ones) are exactly alike. You are a unique creature of God.

Because you are unique, the way you do things must be unique. You cannot be like everybody else and everybody else cannot be like you. Each one of us is unique. This means in ourselves, we are not complete. We need each other to be complete. We are all pieces to complete the jigsaw puzzle. Each piece is critical to making the picture what it is supposed to be.

"Yes, the body has many different parts, not just one part. If the foot says, "I am not a part of the body because I am not a hand," that does not make it any less a part of the body. And if the ear says, "I am not part of the body because I am not an eye," would that make it any less a part of the body? If the whole body were an eye, how would you hear? Or if your whole body were an ear, how would you smell anything? But our bodies have many parts, and God has put each part just where he wants it. How strange a body would be if it had only one part! Yes, there are many parts, but only one body. The eye can never say to the hand, "I don't need you." The head can't say to the feet, "I don't need you." 1 **Corinthians 12:14-21 New Living Translation.**

Understanding the above scripture will give you confidence to be who you have been made to be. It will make you secure and be bold to be the leader God wants you to be. When you understand this, you will be secure to be yourself. When you are secure, then, you can achieve much more.

A secure leader is a better leader. You must be secure in who God has made you to be.

CHAPTERNINE

STRATEGIC PRINCIPLES OF PRUDENCE

*"It takes wisdom to build a house, and understanding
to set it on a firm foundation; It takes knowledge to
furnish its rooms with fine furniture and beautiful
draperies. It's better to be wise than strong; intelligence
outranks muscle any
day. Strategic planning is the key to warfare;
to win, you need a lot of good counsel."*

Proverbs 24:3-6 The Message.

Leadership and wisdom are inseparable twins. You cannot lead without wisdom. Wisdom, the Bible says is the principal thing - it is the major thing. When you solve the wisdom problem, you solve all other problems. Without wisdom, there can be no prominent achievement.

"Above all and before all, do this: Get Wisdom! Write this at the top of your list: Get Understanding! Throw your arms around her—believe me, you won't regret it; Never let her go—she'll make your life glorious." **Proverbs 4:7-8 The Message.**

"Wisdom is of more value than foolishness, just as light is better than darkness." **Ecclesiastes 2:13 Living Bible.**

"For wisdom is far more valuable than rubies. Nothing you desire can compare with it, "I, Wisdom, live together with good judgment. I know where to discover knowledge and discernment. All who fear the LORD will hate evil. Therefore, I hate pride and arrogance, corruption and perverse speech. Common sense and success belong to me. Insight and strength are mine. Because of me, kings reign, and rulers make just decrees. Rulers lead with my help, and nobles make righteous judgments. "I love all who love me. Those who search will surely find me. I have riches and honor, as well as enduring wealth and justice. My gifts are better than gold, even the purest gold, my wages better than sterling silver. I walk in righteousness, in paths of justice. Those who love me inherit wealth. I will fill their treasuries." **Proverbs 8:11-21 New Living Translation.**

"How much better to get wisdom than gold, and good judgment than silver!" **Proverbs 16:16 New Living Translation.**

Wisdom has many sides and many facets. The will of God is that as His children, we should exhibit, exemplify and express His manifold wisdom.

"To the intent that now unto the principalities and powers in heavenly places might be known by the church the manifold wisdom of God." **Ephesians 3:10.**

The phrase manifold means multi-dimensional, multi-faceted and multi-sided. God's purpose is to show His wisdom in rich variety. One of the facets and components of wisdom is prudence. Prudence is being circumspect or discreet. It means "being careful to avoid undesired consequences."

Consequences are the results or the effect of your actions or inactions. Consequences are the harvest of your planting seeds of actions or inactions. Each one is a victim of the consequences he/she has created. Your actions and inactions have resulted in what you are going through now. The present level of your business, career, family, academics, relationships, and indeed your entire life is the direct and indirect consequences of your actions and inactions of yesterday. The seeds planted yesterday have become the harvest of today.

If you are to have a better tomorrow, if you are going to have a better future than your past, then you must learn the strategic principles of prudence. You must be careful to avoid undesired consequences. You must realize that the quality, effectiveness and impact of your life is heavily dependent on the choices you make.

Right choices will lead to right consequences. Wrong choices will lead to wrong consequences. When a man walks in the principles of prudence, he is able to make right choices, which will prevent him from experiencing wrong consequences. A leader must especially be careful because the consequences he faces will not only affect him, but also his followers.

DESIRED AND UNDESIRED CONSEQUENCES

For you as a leader to be prudent (to avoid undesired conse-quences), you have to know the difference between desired and undesired consequences. This is the first step in the strategic principle of prudence. You must know what desired conse-quences you expect and the undesired consequences you want to avoid. If you want to reap mangoes, you must plant mango seeds. You cannot plant orange seeds and expect to reap apples. When you know the desired consequences, then, you can align your actions to ensure the desired consequences are realized. Also, you will be able to align your actions to avoid undesired conse-quences. We can broadly divide desired consequences into two:

General Desired Consequences

The word of God, the Bible, has clearly outlined what general plan/desire/consequence is for us. All you need do is to search the Bible. These consequences have been packaged as promises. Each promise is unlocked by complying with and satisfying the condi-tions therein.

Prudence dictates that a leader, and indeed every Christian, searches the Bible and fulfill all the necessary conditions/actions needed to actualize and appropriate the promises. Acting con-trary to, or not complying with the instructions/commands in the word of God, will lead to undesired consequences. "Don't be misled-you cannot mock the justice of God.

You will always harvest what you plant. Those who live only to satisfy their own sinful nature will harvest decay and death from that sinful nature. But those who live to please the Spirit will harvest everlasting life from the Spirit. So, let's not get tired of doing what is good. At just the right time we will reap a harvest of blessing if we don't give up." Galatians 6:7-9 New Living Translation.

Specific Desired Consequences

There are some specific, specialized personal consequences God desires for your life as an individual and as a leader. God has a specific plan for your life and you must come to the realization that you mean so much to God. God sees you as an individual and has plans that are personal and peculiar to you. You cannot discover God's plan for your life if you do not realize you are very special to Him.

"Casting all your care upon him; for he careth for you." **1 Peter 5:7.**

J.B Philips translation of the last part of this verse puts it as follows: *"…for you are God's personal concern."*

Whatever concerns you is personal to God. God has some personalized plans for your life. You must realize you are not an accident but a deliberate creature of God created for a specific purpose. As a leader, you must understand that you are a creature of purpose, designed on purpose, alive to accomplish purpose.

"You were there while I was being formed in utter seclusion! You saw me before I was born and scheduled each day of my life before I began to breathe. Every day was recorded in your book!" **Psalm 139:15-16 Living Bible.**

In God's mind, there are some desired consequences that He has planned, desired and earmarked for you to walk in as an individual.

"For I know the thoughts that I think toward you, saith the Lord,

thoughts of peace, and not of evil, to give you an expected end." **Jeremiah 29:11.**

You are so important to God and you must realize that your purpose pre-dates you.

"Before I formed thee in the belly I knew thee; and before thou camest forth out of the womb I sanctified thee, and I ordained thee a prophet unto the nations." **Jeremiah 1:5.**

"Listen, O isles, unto me; and hearken, ye people, from far; The Lord hath called me from the womb; from the bowels of my mother hath he made mention of my name. And he hath made my mouth like a sharp sword; in the shadow of his hand hath he hid me, and made me a polished shaft; in his quiver hath he hid me; And said unto me, Thou art my servant, O Israel, in whom I will be glorified" **Isaiah 49:1-3**

"But when it pleased God, who separated me from my mother's womb, and called me by his grace, To reveal his Son in me, that I might preach him among the heathen; immediately I conferred not with flesh and blood." **Galatians 1:15-16.**

Prudence demands you seek what God has in mind for you. When you understand this, you will discover that it becomes your assignment in life. Your leadership will then be purposeful and have a clear direction. This becomes 'the why' of your being alive. Prudence then requires you encapsulate 'your why' into clearly articulated plan. Your desired purpose becomes your vision.

For your vision to be accomplished, that is, for you to have the desired consequences of God realized in your life, you must have goals. Goals are landmarks on your way to accomplishing your vision. Goals are what you want accomplished in realizing your desired vision. Your goals must be specific, attainable, measurable and written down.

Once goals are set, a man who is prudent will develop a plan of action to translate the goals into action. Making plans is not against the word of God. It is when we take God out of our planning that we get into trouble.

"We should make plans--counting on God to direct us." **Proverbs 16:9.**

Working on your goals through a plan of action will produce the desired consequences that you are expecting.

Prudence then, means having a vision, setting goals and having a plan of action.

DON'T NEGOTIATE WITH THE DEVIL

Prudence dictates that you are aware of the likely opposition to having your desired consequences realized.

"A sensible man watches for problems ahead and prepares to meet them. The simpleton never looks and suffers the consequences." **Proverbs 27:12 Living Bible**.

One thing is sure: – the devil is all out to prevent the realization of your desired consequences. Guess what, though? The devil is no match for you, so put him in his right place and move on. In pursuit of your leadership, you will have to overcome mountains, cross rivers and go through valleys but be rest assured that victory is yours!

"For whatsoever is born of God overcometh the world: and this is the victory that overcometh the world, even our faith." **1 John 5:4.**

To overcome means to prevail over, conquer or subdue. All these cannot happen without opposition.

Nowhere in the Bible are we instructed to tolerate, negotiate or compromise with the devil and his manifestations. We are to decisively deal with him.

As a leader you will need to keep cool. Keep a cool head; Stay alert. The devil is poised to pounce, and would like nothing better than to catch you napping; but vigilance and dependence on the Lord is the key.

"Be sober, be vigilant because your adversary, the devil walketh about seeking whom he may devour. Whom resist steadfast in the faith, knowing that the same afflictions are accomplished in your brethren that are in the world. But the God of all grace, who hath called us unto his eternal glory by Christ Jesus, after that ye have suffered a while, make you perfect, stablish, strengthen, settle you." **1Peter 5:8-10.**

PRUDENCE DEMANDS ACQUIRING KNOWLEDGE

Prudence dictates that you have specialized knowledge of whatever you are doing.

"The wise man looks ahead. The fool attempts to fool himself and won't face facts". **Proverbs 14:8 Living Bible.**

Understand the facts/details of your business, career, ministry, subject etc. A prudent man knows exactly what he is doing. A leader without accurate facts is bound to fall.

General knowledge will give you general results. Specialized knowledge will give you specialized results.

As a prudent leader, you must always go the extra mile to acquire the knowledge needed to get your job done very well. This quest for knowledge will make you an expert, specialist and consultant. You must know the what, where, when, how, who of whatever you are involved in. You must know that the rule of the game is to check out every fact, detail and information to ensure you are equipped to arrive at your desired destination.

"Only simpletons believe everything they are told! The prudent carefully consider their steps." **Proverbs 14:15 New Living Translation.**

A leader must be a perpetual student; he must be a wise man, knowing what to do to get his desired results. If he does not have the information he needs, he must know where to get it. Lack of knowledge is dangerous and deadly. It leads to undesired consequences.

"My people are destroyed for lack of knowledge". **Hosea 4:6a.**

"Lest Satan should get an advantage of us: for we are not ignorant of his devices". **2 Corinthians 2:11.**

You cannot divorce prudence from knowledge.

"The simple inherit folly: but the prudent are crowned with knowledge." **Proverbs 14:18.**

"Every prudent man dealeth with knowledge: but a fool layeth open his folly." **Proverbs 13:16.**

"The heart of the prudent getteth knowledge; and the ear of the wise seeketh knowledge." **Proverbs 18:15.**

"Through knowledge shall the righteous be delivered." **Proverbs 11:9b.**

However, having information or knowledge is not an end in itself. The information and knowledge you acquire must be put to proper use. You will need to first understand the information. Understanding answers the question why. Understanding opens your mind to see the meaning, significance and explanation of the information that you have. It is the why that makes you appreciate the value of the information.

When you know the why of the information you have, then, prudence demands you know the how. It is in the how that result resides. It is the how that will empower you to effectively process/apply the information that you have acquired.

"My child, don't lose sight of good planning and in sight. Hang on to them for they fill you with life and bring you honour and respect. They keep you safe on your way and keep your feet from stumbling." **Proverbs 3:21-23 New Living Translation.**

As a leader you must be a prudent man. You must be a wise man with specialist knowledge. A prudent man has common sense, and he forms partnership and teams to assist him succeed.He finds and partners with people who can complement him in his area of weakness. He is a wise planner.

"A house is built by wisdom and become strong through good sense, through knowledge its rooms are filled with all sorts of precious riches and valuables". **Proverbs 24:3-5 Living Bible.**

A prudent man values the importance of wisdom and goes for it.

"Getting wisdom is the most important thing you can do and whatever else you do, get good judgment." **Proverbs 4:7 Living Bible.**

A prudent man neither wastes his words nor does he engage in worthless unprofitable talk. He knows when, where and how to talk. "Answer not a fool according to his folly, lest thou also be like unto him. Answer a fool according to his folly, lest he be wise in his own conceit." **Proverbs 26:4-5.**

"Wise people don't make a show of their knowledge, but fools broadcast their folly". **Proverbs 12:23.**

He doesn't use his knowledge as an instrument of pride. A prudent man knows he cannot share his ideas or dreams with everybody. He knows thoughtless and unguided speech can be dangerous.

"Those who control their tongues will have long life" **Proverbs 13:3b Living Bible.**

"Those who love to talk will experience the consequences for the tongue can kill or nourish life." **Proverbs 18:21 Living Bible.**

If all leaders can acquire and apply the strategic principles of prudence, the world indeed will be a better place. The good news, however, is that this can happen one leader at a time. If you decide to do things the way they ought to be done, then, there is hope.

If you as a leader can operate in the strategic principles of prudence, you will make minimal mistakes. It will help you to have a higher rate of accuracy and leadership success. This is critical because the more accurate a leader is, the deeper his leadership influence will be. A leader who makes too many mistakes and errors of judgement will soon be replaced or disgraced from office. The strategic principles of prudence promotes excellence across the team.

72

Life is all about relationships. Leadership is about people; hence relationship is a critical issue. Every rational human being has a deep hunger for beneficial relationships. Human beings survive and thrive best when they are involved in meaningful relationships. This is especially true for a leader because if care is not taken, a leader can get to the point where he is isolated from people. The tragedy of many leaders is that the few people whom they have relationships with are either bootleggers or sycophants.

Relationship is the way in which two or more people are connected. It is the state of being connected. It is the way in which two or more people or a group relate towards each other. Without meaningful and strategic relationships, life will be full of frustration. You will not be able to maximize your leadership potentials without the vital role of relationship.

Life is a web of relationships and this can either be positive or negative. Relationship is the vehicle upon which influence travels. Human beings are daily being influenced through relationships. Your beliefs and actions are daily being affected by the people you relate and interact with.

Everybody has the capacity to be influenced or to influence because man is a social animal. The quality of your life is heavily dependent on the quality of your relationships. If you are a businessman, the relationship between you and your customers influences your line of goods and your approach to business. Your relationship with your customers determines whether they will continue to patronize you or not; it determines whether they will recommend you to others or deter them from coming to you. Your relationship with them has a direct effect on their actions and beliefs (remember influence is the ability to affects somebody's actions or beliefs). Your relationship with those who have gotten you into trouble in the past will influence how you will relate to others who you think have the potential to cause you trouble and pain - once beaten, twice shy.

Due to the serious consequence(s) of relationships, you have to be very selective on the relationships you crave for and cultivate. No relationship is neutral so you cannot afford to be too close or intimate with everybody. Your life is too crucial to be negatively influenced. Your destiny is too precious to be polluted with destructive influences. No relationship is neutral. There is always an exchange of influence in every relationship. Every relationship is a carrier of influence. You are either influencing the other party or the other party is influencing you. As a leader, there are some relationships that you have to be very careful not to allow to become intimate.

Relationships that do not bring out the best in you should not be consciously cultivated. A good relationship should stretch you. It should challenge and motivate you to be a better person – a better businessman, a better student, a better husband, a better wife, a better citizen, a better Christian, a better leader.

Never encourage or allow relationships that tolerate mediocrity in your life. Never invest time in relationships that do not demand excellence from you.

Any relationship that does not enhance the execution of God's purpose for your life must be avoided, else it derails you from God's plan.

"He that walketh with wise men shall be wise: but a companion of fools shall be destroyed." **Proverbs 13:20.**

Avoid and run away from relationships that lure you into sin, mediocrity, compromise and bad habits. These relationships have a tendency to drag you down.

"Keep away from angry, short-tempered people or you will learn to be like them and endanger your soul." **Proverbs 22: 24 New Living Translation.**

The Bible warns us to avoid having relationships with gossips.

"A gossip tells secrets so don't hang around with someone who talks too much." **Proverbs 20:19 New Living Translation.**

KEEP FOOLS AT BAY

You must avoid having relationships with fools. Nobody wants to be called a fool but many times, people do things which qualify them to be so described. Fools are known by their thoughts, words and actions and the bible talks a lot about fools. Let us look at seven of the characteristics of fools outlined in the bible. People who constantly exhibit (and refuse to be helped to change) these traits and characteristics are not people you should encourage to be in your circle of influence.

1. Fools are prone to anger and are quarrelsome.

"Avoiding a fight is a mark of honour, only fools insist on quarrelling." **Proverbs 20:3 New Living Translation.**

"Fools get into constant quarrels." **Proverbs 18:6 New Living Translation.**

Unnecessary arguments, unbridled anger and unwarranted disagreements are symptoms of the presence of a fool. Actually the bible says "anger rests in the bosom of fools." Ecclesiastes 7:9. A translation of that verse puts it as "anger is the friend of fools."

2. Fools waste their time and squander opportunities.

". . . only fools idle away their time." **Proverbs 12:11B New Living Translation.**

"So be careful how you live, not as fools but as those who are wise. Make the most of every opportunity for doing good in these evil days." **Ephesians 5:15**.

Time is a commodity every human being has in the same measure (twenty-four hours) and the way you utilize this product goes a long way in determine what your lot in life will be. Fools waste time, not realizing that it is perishable and can never be recycled.

3. Fools have no investments.

"The wise have wealth and luxury but fools spend whatever they get" **Proverbs 21:20 New Living Translation.**

To live life oblivious of tomorrow is one of the greatest acts of folly. Savings and investments are the things which give us a soft landing for the future. A fool lives for today and foolishly thinks that tomorrow will take care of itself.

4. Fools don't investigate facts before making a decision/judgment.

"Wise people think before they act, fools don't and even brag about it." **Proverbs 13:16 New Living Translation.**

"What a shame, what folly to give advice before listening to the facts." **Proverbs 18:13 New Living Translation.**

As a leader, you need friends and associates who will be thorough. You need people around you who don't just accept whatever they are told or whatever they see without thinking. You need people who investigate facts before making decisions and judgments. It is foolishness to jump into conclusions before hearing the other side.

"Any story sounds true until someone tells the other side and sets the records straight." **Proverbs 18:17 Living Bible.**

5. Fools Slander People

" he that publishes an ill-report the same is a fool" **Proverbs 10:18 New Living Translation.**

Whenever you see anybody talking ill of people without justification, be careful because that person is on the slippery road to folly.

Fools insist on their own opinion. You do not want to closely associate with people who will not listen to you or take into consideration other people's advice. You need to cultivate relationships with people who listen, evaluate and consider other people's opinions.

"Fools have no interest in understanding; they only want to air their own opinions." **Proverbs 18:2 New Living Translation.**

Fools think they need no advice.

"Fools think they need no advice but the wise listen to others." **Proverbs 12:15 New Living Translation.**

You must not only know what relationships to avoid, you must also know what relationships to cultivate

IT DOESN'T JUST HAPPEN

A good relationship does not just happen; it takes hard work. Time and effort must be invested to acquire, nurture and grow relationships. It takes a conscious effort and hard work to maximize the potential in every relationship. Relationships must not be static. You will need to regularly assess, review and service your relationships. Relationships don't just happen.

"A man that hath friends must shew himself friendly: and there is a friend that sticketh closer than a brother." **Proverbs 18:24.**

To have meaningful relationships, you cannot be static; you have to shift. You have to either get close to people or allow people to get close to you. You cannot be a recluse and expect to develop meaningful relationships. You cannot be in your shell and expect that you will have meaningful relationships. You should network with leaders in your field. Join associations that are relevant to your area of specialization. Do what you can to reach out to form meaningful relationships and partnerships.

"The most important single ingredient in the formula of success is knowing how to get along with people." Theodore Roosevelt.

Diligence plays a crucial role in the formation of some strategic relationships. When a leader is diligent, he attracts some relationships that will enhance or even change his status.

"Seest thou a man diligent in his business? He shall stand before kings, he shall not stand before mean men". **Proverbs 22:29.**

Mean men are poor in character, low in status. When you are diligent in whatever you do, you will be promoted from relating with men of low status to relating with kings. As you stand before kings, you develop new relationships and your influence increases. For example, a shop owner who is diligent in every dimension of his business and offers the best service in town, will most likely attract the best customers. If his shop is patronized by celebrities, he becomes a man of influence due to his celebrity clients and customers.

Developing, nurturing and maintaining the right relationships is a vital tool to the success of a leader. Your next promotion might just be a relationship away.

When we talk of relationships, it is on two levels. You need to develop relationships with people "above" you and with people "below" you. You need people above you to motivate, challenge and inspire you to move up higher. These relationships should inspire you to want to do more and be better than you are doing.

You must also be able to motivate, challenge and inspire people under you to also come up. You must have an eye to discover, develop and maximize critical relationships. The Lord will divinely link you up with strategic people at strategic times and you must be sensitive to know the mind of God.

You must learn to court relationships that will move you forward in God. You must know how to develop relationships with people that have a track record of truly following God. You must relate with people who are models of the life God desires for you; people who do not only talk the talk, but also walk the walk. You must cherish relationship with people who have duly paid their dues and paid the price to reach where they are. Apostle Paul, indeed, paid his dues and was worthy of being followed.

"Be ye followers of me, even as I also am of Christ." **1Corinthians11:1.**

"For though ye have ten thousand instructors in Christ, yet have ye not many fathers: for in Christ Jesus I have begotten you through the gospel. Wherefore I beseech you, be ye followers of me." 1 **Corinthians 4:15-16.**

"Brethren, be followers together of me, and mark them which walk so as ye have us for an ensample." **Philippians 3:17.**

"And ye became followers of us, and of the Lord, having received the word in much affliction, with joy of the Holy Ghost. So that ye were en-samples to all that believe in Macedonia and Achaia." **Thessalonians 1:6.**

The quality of your relationships will determine the quality of your life and the quality of your life will determine the quality of your leadership.

CHAPTER ELEVEN

INDICES OF A GOOD LEADER

"A leader of good judgment gives stability: an exploiting leader leaves a trail of waste."

Proverbs 29:4 The Message.

Many people today claim and pride themselves to be leaders but their impact is neither positive nor progressive. Leadership is not all about title, status, office, position, pomp and pageantry and all the paraphernalia attached to it. Leadership is simply influence influencing a specific group of people to achieve and accomplish a specific purpose. Leadership is not just an appellation. It is about helping people.

Leadership is about having a positive and lasting impact on the lives of people. Leadership is about making people's lives better than it was when you first met them.

A good leader is a performer. He understands the purpose for which he is chosen as a leader and he gets the job done. He progressively takes his followers to accomplish the purpose of their individual and corporate existence.

A good leader knows "the why" the organization is set up. He is actively pursuing that purpose and getting results. He is able to identify what needs to be done and he mobilizes men and marshals resources to get the job done.

A good leader is a person of influence. Manipulation, control, deceit and bullying are strange words to him.

"A good leader motivates, doesn't mislead, doesn't exploit." **Proverbs 16:10 The Message.**

His presence instils confidence and he encourages the people to get involved in tasks that will enhance corporate good. He is courageous. He is bold. He is a pacesetter. He acts on his convictions. He has the guts and the liver to do the right thing every time, no matter whose ox is gored. He never abdicates responsibility to pressure, problems or people who don't believe in his leadership.

A good leader is faithful, loyal and honest. He takes responsibility for the state of the people he is leading. He is loyal to his team and to his people. He defends them. He protects them. He promotes their interest. He does not take credit for helping the people he is called to serve. A good leader is committed to the welfare of his followers. He never allows his followers to be taken for granted. The people he is leading come first before anything else. He is all out to serve the interest of his followers and he never compromises nor does he mortgage their interest for anything. He is reliable.

When he fails, he is honest and man enough to admit his mistake. When he is praised, he does not let it get into his head. He is not into demanding honour, respect and accolades.

"It's not good to eat too much honey, and it's not good to seek honors for yourself." **Proverbs 25:27 New Living Translation.**

He does not change his plans and strategies without adequate thought to the effect on the corporate interest of those he is leading. He knows his actions or inactions will affect his followers one way or the other.

A good leader is not someone who has all the answers or who does all the thinking but he is an honest person who will do everything to help his followers get the answers they need.

A good leader is not a perfect man. He is not the person that does the entire job but someone who facilitates the job to be done.

He is not someone who stands aloof but he is a man of the people, who is all out to ensure their best interest. A good leader is not surrounded by sycophants. He is strong enough to have real, honest and bold people around him. A good leader never tolerates evil.

"Good leaders abhor wrongdoing of all kinds; sound leadership has a moral foundation." **Proverbs 16:12 The Message.**

A leader knows he is accountable first to God and then, to the people he is leading. A good leader is a person of integrity.

"Love and truth form a good leader; sound leadership is founded on

loving integrity." **Proverbs 20:28 The Message.**

"People with integrity have firm footing but those who follow crooked paths will slip and fall." **Proverbs 10:9 New Living Translation.**

A leader has something to offer. He has capacity to do things. He is gifted. He is talented. He is skilled. He has relevant exposure, experience and expertise.

A leader is a pacesetter. He sets the pace for his followers. He is their role model. They listen to him. They respect him. They look up to him. They take his opinion serious and his advice is valued. The leader is an inspiration. He fills his followers with the desire and drive to get the purpose of the group and their lives actualized. A leader is effective. He accomplishes the purpose for which God has placed him as a leader. He is a man who is an epitome of competence and character. He is indeed a leader worthy of emulation by other leaders.

ABOUT THE BOOK

The world is experiencing leadership crisis in virtually every segment of human endeavour. The problem is compounded by the seeming scarcity of truly dedicated, mentally sound and effective leaders. This scarcity has created a vacuum and untold needless hardship which need not be so. People are longing for leaders with the critical ingredients of integrity, faithfulness and forthright character who will deliver the dividends of leadership and make life easier and better. This indeed, are critical times where leadership matters must not be taken lightly or with levity. They are critical matters that demand critical attention.

LEADERSHIP MATTERS is a book on leadership and its various components. In this book, we find how being inquisitive can make the difference between success and failure, survival or going under, profit or loss, strangulation or expansion; and how answering critical life questions can help to attain effective leadership. It also explains the principles of prudence as well as the importance of building good relationships to achieve leadership success. Here, we examine the challenges associated with leadership and how to stay on the path against all odds. Leadership can indeed be a daunting task but this book helps to simplify it to make it an achievable task.

ABOUT THE AUTHOR

Tunde Jaiyebo is the Senior Pastor of Charis Family International Church. Pastor Jaiyebo attended University of Ife, Ile-Ife, Oyo State, Nigeria (now Obafemi Awolowo University, Osun State, Nigeria) where he bagged an honours degree in Law.

After graduating from the Nigeria Law School in Lagos, Nigeria, he practiced as a Legal Practitioner for several years.

Pastor Jaiyebo now devotes his full time to teaching, writing, pastoring and leadership development. He has written over eleven books and is a columnist in Sunday Tribune, a national daily in Nigeria.

He is happily married to Mojisola Jaiyebo, a co-labourer in the work of the ministry and they are blessed with two children (Toluwanimi and Mofifoluwa).

OTHER LEADERSHIP BOOKS BY THEAUTHOR

* Effective Leadership

* Leadership Manual

* Leadership Pocketbook

*A-Z of effective Leadership

OTHER BOOKS FROMCHARIS MEDIA HOUSE

NO WAY MR. DEVIL

YOUR LIFE COUNTS

THANK GOD, YESTERDAY ENDED LAST NIGHT

FOOLS AND WHAT THEY DO

LAZYBONES AND WHAT THEY DO

ANGRY PEOPLE AND WHAT THEY DO

PROUD PEOPLE AND WHAT THEY DO

HELP! MY PRAYERS ARE NOT WORKING

THANK GOD FOR POTIPHAR'S WIFE

FORGIVENESS101

GUILT

USE OR MISS IT

WORRY

REJECTION